A Perspective o

A history of Pend

by Bob Little

Published and available from
TheEndlessBookcase.com
This booklet is available in both paper and electronic format.
Available in multiple e-book formats
The Endless Bookcase Ltd
71 Castle Road, St Albans ,Hertfordshire
England, UK, AL1 5DQ

First edition: July 2014. Reprinted: September 2014
ISBN: 978-1-908941-35-0

About the Author

Bob Little has pursued a number of parallel careers but he is best known as a writer, commentator and publicist. He's also a blogger and broadcaster - and even, at times, a speaker and singer. His work is published in the UK, Continental Europe, the USA, South America and Australia. You can find out more about him by visiting www.boblittlepr.com

As a boy, Bob saw one of Shakespeare's plays performed at Pendley Manor, as part of the annual Shakespeare Festival. The whole experience that summer's evening long ago, which included seeing the Manor's then owner, Dorian Williams, play a cameo part in the play – on horseback - left a deep, lasting and highly positive impression. As a result, Bob has always had a 'soft spot' for Pendley.

After being given the chance to write a couple of magazine articles about Pendley, Bob was asked to research and then write a history of the Manor and the people associated with it over the centuries. The result is this book.

Researching the book, writing it and bringing the whole project to fruition has been a time-travelling adventure. It has offered intriguing and sometimes enlightening glimpses into various historical periods - along with an idea of the part that Pendley played in influencing those periods. The research has revealed fascinating insights into the characters, now long dead, who have shaped the Manor's history. Hopefully, this book will yield up at least some of these insights to its readers.

Acknowledgements

My thanks are due to members of the Tring and District Local History and Museum Society which runs the Tring Museum, especially to Tim Amsden, Mike Bass, Shelley Savage and John Savage who have provided a wealth of valuable information and pictures for this book. In addition, I'm grateful to the photographer, Andrea Moore, who has also contributed some pictures to this book. I'm also delighted that members of the Williams' family have given their permission for Williams' family photographs to be included in this book.

Grateful thanks are also due to Angharad Little, currently Head of History at Verulam School, St Albans, who provided invaluable assistance in critiquing and commenting on the research underpinning this book and to Helen Little, a highly skilled genealogist, who helped with the preparation of this book in many ways – not least in pursuing a great deal of painstaking research in order to identify the people in the Williams' family photographs that help to illustrate this book.

Thanks, too, to David Roberts who, when he was the General Manager at Pendley Manor, had the idea for this book in the first place.

Contents

About the Author ii

Acknowledgements.. iii

Welcome to Pendley Manor 1

The early years: Britons and Romans 4

Anglo-Saxons and Normans... 7

The Wars of the Roses and the Rise of the Verneys 14

Minor issues.. 17

Intrigue, plots and conspiracies 21

A ghostly Cavalier.. 26

Origin of a President... 29

A new family – and a new Manor House............................... 31

The last Williams at Pendley... 51

A Residential Centre of Adult Education 60

Christmas at Pendley.. 67

A new regime – and characters.. 70

Up to now 78

Pendley's Shakespeare connection...................................... 87

Appendix: A personal perspective of Pendley 100

Welcome to Pendley Manor

If you're reading this, then the chances are that you're at Pendley Manor. Alternatively, you're thinking about visiting it or, perhaps, you've visited it and want to be reminded of your time there. All of these are laudable and, potentially, enjoyable situations to be in.

Hopefully – if you're about to come to, or are at, Pendley - this guide will help to put much of what you find in the house and its estate into a helpful context.

The last private individual to own and live at Pendley Manor was Dorian Williams. For many years, he was the BBC's voice of televised show jumping. His last broadcast was in 1985, just a few months before he died, aged 71.

On his death, Pendley's grade II listed country house and its 35 acres of grounds passed into commercial hands.

The Manor House – now patrolled by a number of imperious and self-absorbed peacocks – has become an award winning (including two rosettes for its restaurant), four-star country manor house, with 73 double bedded rooms, a ballroom for up to 200 guests and a spa with swimming pool and snooker room.

It caters for conferences (up to 250 people), banquets, weddings and civil partnership celebrations. From personal experience, it can also offer a delicious afternoon tea.

From personal experience, Pendley can provide a delicious afternoon tea.

The estate's first manor house was built in the 15ᵗʰ century.

The current house dates from the 1870s and is only the second manor house to have been built on the ancient settlement of Pendley – variously spelled, over the years, as Penley, Pendele and Pentlai.

From Ancient Britons to a BBC show jumping commentator, via ambitious mediaeval nobility, and even the ancestors of a famous President of the USA, a great many people have shaped the Pendley we know today. The following pages endeavour to explain...

By Bob Little

Opening a door on Pendley Manor....

The early years: Britons and Romans

The village of Pendley is first recorded in the fourth century – bordered, to the south, by Akeman Street (the Roman road which runs from just north of St Albans to Cirencester); with the pre-Roman Icknield Way only half a mile to the north.

As Roman rule in Britain faded – in the fifth century - there is some evidence that a British tribe, under the kingship of Cynwyd, son of Cynfelin who was the youngest son of King Arthwys of the Pennines, moved into the area.

Although the British kingdoms in the north and west of Britain were well established by the turn of the fifth century, the structure of the south and east is much less certain.

Some of the descendants of the northern king, Coel Hen (350 – 420AD), appear to have moved south into this potential vacuum and made their mark on the Midlands of Britain, probably once the Romano-British central administration had collapsed.

Coel Hen – which translates into English as 'Old King Cole' - may have been one of the last of the Roman Duces Brittanniarum (Dukes of the Britons) who commanded the Roman army.

He is said to have become a King of the Britons following the reign of King Asclepiodotus. Upset with Asclepiodotus's policies and decisions, which brought hardship to many of his people, Coel began a rebellion in the duchy of Caer Colun (thought to be Colchester) – which could be a reason why

Britons from the north, under Coel's jurisdiction, came to the area we now know of as Hertfordshire and Essex.

Coel met Asclepiodotus in battle and killed him, thus taking the kingship of Britain for himself. Rome sent a senator, Constantius Chlorus, to negotiate with Coel. Coel agreed to pay tribute and submit to Roman laws as long as he was allowed to retain the kingship. Constantius agreed to these terms but, one month later, Coel died[1].

Among those Britons who came south during this time is said to be Cynfelyn, the youngest son of King Arthwys of the Pennines – and, apparently, he established control of an area in the southern Midlands. His son, Cynwyd, found willing followers in the Chiltern Hills where he set up the kingdom of Cynwidion.

Later, these people – then ruled by Cynwyd's son, Cadrod - changed their tribal name to 'Calchwynedd', taking their

---

[1] Incidentally, there is a romantic rumour that Constantius married Coel's daughter, Helena, and crowned himself as Coel's successor. Subsequently, Helena gave birth to a son who was to become the Emperor Constantine the Great, giving a British pedigree to the Roman imperial line.

However, Coel Hen lived from 350 – 420AD but Constantine the Great died in 337AD and, so, was dead before Coel Hen was born. Thus the British Helena couldn't have been Constantine's mother.

Constantine's parents are recorded as being Constantius Caesar and his common law wife, Helena, who was from Asia Minor and was described as a 'stabularia', or barmaid. However, Constantius Caesar died in York, in 306AD; so his son, Constantine, acceded to the Imperial throne 'from Britain' – but still had nothing to do with Coel Hen.

name from the area's limestone/chalk hills (since 'calch' is British/ Welsh for 'lime').

Tradition ascribes this kingdom to an area which now includes the towns of Northampton and Dunstable. It may well have occupied the former heartland of the Catuvellauni tribe, especially in its later days, when this appears to have been compressed towards the south by the invading Angles.

Archaeological evidence indicates that the British held out here well into the seventh century.

Anglo-Saxons and Normans

The invading Anglo-Saxons took over the Pendley area at some point after 630AD. Eventually, these Chiltern Saxons – who were under Mercian rule - became subsumed into the kingdom of the West Saxons but not before a seventh century Saxon nobleman, Penda of Mercia, had probably given his name to the Pendley area.

Penda's military campaigns and his unlikely alliance with the British king, Cadwallon, were instrumental in making Mercia an independent kingdom and establishing its prestige and power in Dark Age Britain. In his 'Historia Ecclesiastica Gentis Anglorum', written in the early eighth century, Bede of Jarrow describes Penda as 'a barbarian more savage than any pagan' with 'no respect for the newly established religion of Christ'. And in the ninth-century 'Historia Brittonum', Nennius describes Penda as 'victorious through the arts of the Devil, for he was not baptised and never believed in God'.

On his accession to the throne of Mercia in 633, Penda sought to conquer the other Anglo-Saxon kingdoms. Over the next 22 years Penda, England's last great heathen king, killed the Christian kings Edwin, Oswald, Oswin, Ecgric and Sigebert. Apparently, he also killed Anna, King of the East Angles. Penda died at the battle of Windwaed in 655. It is said that he was aged 80 when he died and that this was an appropriate and honourable end for a pagan warrior of the time. If Penda did die in battle, aged 80, he was a remarkably strong octogenarian. He was also surprisingly and impressively vigorous since, apparently, he was survived by his three year old son.

The last Anglo-Saxon in charge of the Pendley area – in 1066 - was a nun, called Eddeva (or Edeva), who administered the estate (that is, was said to be Lord of Pendley) on behalf of an Anglo-Saxon called Engelric, who is described as a priest. Engelric seems to have been Lord of Dunsley and Upper Dunsley in the Tring area in 1066, as well as Overlord of Gubblecote, Wigginton, Tring and Pendley – all within the Tring area. Perhaps unsurprisingly, Engelric did not retain these titles after 1066. In those pre-Conquest days, the centrepiece of the manor of Pendley was said to be the convent over which Eddeva presided.

After the Norman Conquest – and certainly by 1086, when the Domesday Book was compiled - the manor of Pendley was owned by Robert, Earl of Mortain and the manor was placed within the 'hundred' of Tring. Among other things, Robert had been given 'two hides of land in the manor' as part of his reward for supporting his relation, the conquering William, who was offered the crown of England in Berkhamsted, just a few miles away from Pendley.

In Berkhamsted, William – having won the Battle of Hastings and then having crossed the River Thames at Wallingford - was met by a delegation of the English establishment. He accepted the surrender of the English, led by Aetheling Edgar - the heir to King Harold II's English claim to the throne – along with Archbishop Aldred, Earl Edwin, Earl Morcar and the chief men of London, who swore their loyalty to William. William was offered the crown there but, instead, William opted to accept the keys to London in Berkhamsted and said that he would accept the crown of England in London. So, it was in Berkhamsted that William of Normandy became William the Conqueror. On Christmas Day in 1066, William was crowned William I of England in Westminster Abbey. A local legend refers to Berkhamsted as the 'real capital of England' - if only for a few minutes.

The Domesday Book records: 'In Pendley, [Robert] the Count [of Mortain] holds 2 hides himself. Land for 2 Ploughs. 1 villager with 6 smallholders have 1 plough; another possible. Meadow for 1½ ploughs. Value 30s; when acquired 20s; before 1066, 40s. The nun Edeva held this land from Engelric; she could not grant it. These 2 hides are of the 7 hides which the Count of Mortain took in Tring.'

Robert - a half-brother of William the Conqueror (who was born around 1028) - was the son of Herluin de Conteville and Herleva of Falaise (William the Conqueror's mother). Robert was born around 1031, in Normandy, and was probably not more than a year or so younger than his brother, Odo, of Bayeux.

Around 1049, William – who was ruling Normandy as William II - made Robert the Count of Mortain and entrusted to him the key duty of guarding Normandy's borders with Brittany and Bellême. In 1066, Robert agreed to provide 120 ships for William's invasion fleet, which was more than any other of William's supporters.

Robert is one of the few people who are known to have been at the Battle of Hastings in 1066. The Bayeux Tapestry depicts him at a dinner at Pevensey, seated with his brothers, William and Odo, on the day of the landing in England.

William regarded Robert's contribution to the success of the invasion as highly significant and so he awarded him a large share of the spoils. The Domesday Book shows Robert owning 797 manors in 20 counties. The overall worth of his estates was £2,100.

In 1069, along with Robert of Eu, Robert – who tended to base himself in Somerset when he was in England - led an army to victory against a force of Danes in Lindsay. After that, he appears to have been an absentee landholder, spending the majority of his time in Normandy.

At the beginning of the 13th century, William de Bocland owned the manor. It may have come to him through his marriage to Maud, the daughter of William de Say. When William de Bocland died, his heirs were his three daughters: Maud, the wife of William de Averanges; Hawisia, the wife of John de Bovill, and Joan, the wife of Robert de Ferrers. On the partition of his manors, in 1218/19, Pendley went to Hawisia.

Towards the middle of that century, the manor came into the possession of Roger, the son of John de Messeworthe. Before 1290, it had passed to Adam Aignel (sometimes spelled 'de Aignell' or 'de Angle'). From Adam's son, John, the manor went to Adam's great-grandson, John - who was one of the first Members of Parliament and who died in 1361, leaving only an infant son (also – with a stoical disregard for originality - called John). While still a minor, this John Aignel married one of the daughters of Sir John de la Hay. The (young) John Aignel's widowed mother, Katherine married Andrew de Bures, and she and her husband occupied the manor during the heir's minority. John Aignel held the manor in 1378, and granted a rent from it, in 1385/86, to Thomas Peyure.

By 1401/02, the manor had passed to two of Sir John de la Hay's daughters. Initially it was controlled by Joan, who married Walter Pain and, later, John Impey. In 1405 Joan and John Impey settled half the manor on themselves along with their daughter, Joan, and her heirs, with the remainder left in default to Richard Pain and his sisters, Isabel and Eleanor – who were children of Joan by her first husband. A further conveyance was made by them, in 1414, to Walter Salford and others.

As a result of these conveyances, a legal action was brought against Joan and John by Robert Whittingham (sometimes spelled Whytingham) - who had married de la Hay's other daughter, Alice. Robert Whittingham, whose family is said, by some, to have held responsible positions at the court of King Edward III (1312 – 1377), claimed the whole manor and appears to have won his case.

Robert and Alice's son, also called Robert, and his wife, Agnes, inherited the manor in 1440. In that year, Robert Whittingham, who had been Sheriff of the county in 1438, obtained 'free warren in the manor' (allowing him to snare rabbits) and was granted a licence to enclose 200 acres in the parish for a park. This enabled him to destroy the town of Pendley to create a park and build the first manor house. This trend – of enclosing areas in Hertfordshire as estates for large houses – had started around 1400. By 1485, there were some 40 substantial parks in Hertfordshire, of which Pendley was one.

A document dating from 1506 states that, some 80 years earlier (in the days of Robert and Alice Whittingham), Pendley was 'a great town, whereof part lay in the parish of Tring and part in the parish of Aldbury. The part in the parish of Tring was held of the Archbishop of Canterbury as of his manor of Tring and the part in the parish of Aldbury of the manor of Aldbury. At that time there was no great

11

mansion house there but there were, in the town, eight fairly large dwellings and eight crofts. It offered work for 'at least 13 ploughs besides divers handicraft men, as tailors, shoemakers and cardmakers with divers others. The town was afterwards cast down and laid to pasture by Sir Robert Whittingham, who built the said place at the west end there as the town sometimes stood, for the town was in the east and south part of the same place.'

This lost village of Pendley lay between what is now Station Road and London Road.

It also appears that Sir Robert Whittingham also ploughed up a common way but, in 1491/92, vestiges of the town's ancient hedges still remained.

Sir Robert's manor house was noted for having a double courtyard. It was also reputed to have had a cloistered inner court, such as can be seen in contemporary buildings including Herstmonceux Castle, Ockwells and Eton College. Whittingham's manor house stood slightly to the east of the present house. That house burnt down in 1835 and was destroyed completely in 1847. So no trace of it now survives.

Whittingham's manor house – which was destroyed in 1847 - stood slightly to the east of the present house (pictured). No trace of it survives.

The Wars of the Roses and the Rise of the Verneys

Whittingham appeared to have chosen his royal allegiance unwisely – supporting Henry VI during the Wars of the Roses.

Consequently, in 1461, Edward IV granted the manor first to George, Bishop of Exeter, for life; then to Thomas Montgomery (also in 1461); to Henry Bourchier, the Earl of Essex (in 1467), and, in 1469, to George, the Archbishop of York.

When Edward IV fled to Flanders in 1470, Henry VI returned to the throne.

He re-instated Sir Robert Whittingham's family at Pendley in 1472 – in consideration for the services he had received from Sir Ralph Verney.

Ralph was the father of John Verney, who had married Robert Whittingham's daughter and heiress, Margaret.

Margaret and Sir John, as he later became, inherited the manor – subject to Thomas Montgomery's life interest in the property.

In the nearby Aldbury parish church – of St John the Baptist – stands the altar tomb of Sir Robert Whittingham. The sides of the tomb are panelled and bear the arms of Whittingham, Verney and Bray.

The tomb of Sir Robert Whittingham and his wife, Agnes. Photograph by Andrea Moore, reproduced by permission.

The tomb was brought to Aldbury with its enclosing stone screens from the church of the suppressed house of Bonhommes at Ashridge, in 1575, by Edmund Verney.

On it lie stone effigies of Sir Robert Whittingham and his wife. Sir Robert is fully armed in plate with mail hauberk and wears a collar of S.S. (a Lancastrian order) and a short surcoat, on which are the arms of Whittingham.

His head rests on a helm which has lost its crest but retains the crest wreath and, at his feet, is a wild man with a club. His wife's feet rest on a hind.

Sir Robert was killed at the battle of Tewkesbury, during the Wars of the Roses, in 1471.

The tomb of Sir Robert Whittingham and his wife, Agnes – showing the
wild man and the hind foot rests. Photograph by Andrea Moore,
reproduced by permission.

The Verney family can be traced, in Buckinghamshire – a
neighbouring county to Hertfordshire - from the 13th
century. The family's earliest property - at Middle Claydon
- was acquired by the first Sir Ralph Verney about 1467.

Subsequently, his son, Sir John Verney, acquired Pendley
Manor, which was just across the Hertfordshire border.
Thereafter the family continued to prosper although its
successive heads were short-lived.

Minor issues

Sir John Verney served as Sheriff of Hertfordshire (in 1499) and Essex and is thought to have been buried in All Saints' Church in nearby Kings Langley, in 1505. Margaret survived him.

Pendley Manor passed, on John's death, to his son, Ralph – who eventually became Sir Ralph Verney.

Ralph Verney, whose wife was Maid of Honour to the English Queen, Catherine of Aragon, was present at The Field of the Cloth of Gold, or Camp du Drap d'Or - a place in Balinghem, between Guînes and Ardres, in France, near Calais, which was the site of a meeting that took place, from 7th June to 24th June 1520, between King Henry VIII of England and King Francis I of France. The meeting was arranged to increase the bond of friendship between the two kings following the Anglo-French treaty of 1514.

Ralph Verney died in 1525, before his son and heir, also called Ralph, had 'come of age' legally.

This Sir Ralph Verney (1509 – 1546), the fourth person in the family to bear that name, married – in 1528 – Elizabeth Bray (1513 – 1573), the daughter of the first Lord Bray, of Eaton Bray in Bedfordshire.

Continuing the Verneys' connection with Henry VIII's wives, this Ralph Verney was given the job of bringing Anne of Cleves to England.

Brass to the memory of Sir Ralph Verney (died 1546), his wife Elizabeth
(Bray) and their 12 children - nine sons and three daughters.
Photograph by Andrea Moore, reproduced by permission.

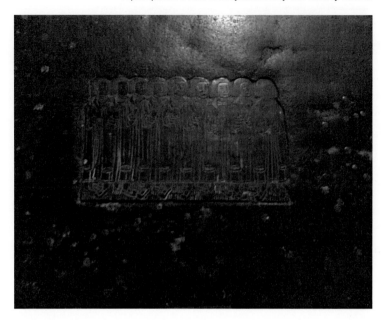

A detail from the brass showing Sir Ralph Verney and his wife Elizabeth (Bray)'s nine sons. Photograph by Andrea Moore, reproduced by permission.

They had 12 children and, on Ralph's death in April 1546, at the age of 37, the manor came to his son, Edmund – who was 18 years old and so, like his father, inherited the manor as a minor.

St John the Baptist church in Albury, the next village to Pendley, contains a tomb, into the slab of which are inlaid bass figures of Sir Ralph Verney and his wife, Elizabeth (Bray), with nine sons and three daughters.

Sir Ralph wears a tabard with the arms of Verney quartering the second Verney coat and Whittingham. His wife bears on her mantle the same arms, together with the Bray quarterings.

Brass in St John the Baptist Church, Aldbury, showing Sir Ralph Verney wearing a tabard with the arms of Verney quartering the second Verney coat and Whittingham. His wife, Elizabeth, bears on her mantle the same arms, together with the Bray quarterings. Photograph by Andrea Moore, reproduced by permission.

Of a landed estate valued at £330 a year, Edmund Verney inherited one third, including the manors of Pendley and Claydon (which had been leased by the Giffords), a flock of 900 ewes and the household goods at Pendley.

Edmund's wardship, first acquired by the second Earl of Rutland, was bought - in 1546 - by Sir Edward Peckham, of Denham in Buckinghamshire. Edward Peckham's daughter, Dorothy, married Edmund Verney in 1546. She died in childbirth in May 1547 but her father retained custody of the property until November 1549, when Edmund Verney 'came of age'.

Intrigue, plots and conspiracies

Edmund Verney's second wife was almost certainly a member of the Knyvet family. In October 1551, Edmund granted the site of Pendley Manor to Anthony Knyvet (c1507 – 1st March 1554).

Sir Anthony Knyvet (or Knyvett), a courtier during the reign of King Henry VIII, was born in London, the son of Charles Knyvett, who was in the retinue of the Duke of Norfolk and Lord Berners, the Deputy of Calais. Sir Anthony was Lieutenant of the Tower of London and is mentioned in Foxe's 'Book of Martyrs' for refusing to continue torturing the Protestant, Anne Askew, on the rack. He became Governor of Portsmouth in 1544 and oversaw the building of Southsea Castle in that year. In 1554, he joined Wyatt's Rebellion, which was ended at the Battle of Hartley. He was executed at the Tower of London on 1st March 1554. Following Anthony Knyvet's execution for treason, the bond given to him by Edmund Verney in 1553 was transferred to Richard Knyvet. Subsequently Edmund Verney's wife, Alice, appeared as one of the remaindermen in a property settlement made by Richard Knyvet, in 1556.

From the outset of their careers, Edmund Verney and his brother, Francis, moved in Protestant circles. It was probably their uncle, the second Lord Bray, who introduced them at court. Their more distant kinsman, John Dudley, later the Duke of Northumberland, passed most of the month of July 1548 at Pendley.

In May 1551, the two Verneys were among the large entourage accompanying the Marquess of Northampton on his embassy to France. In the same year, the Marquess of

Northampton became Lord Lieutenant of Buckinghamshire. These connexions explain not only the two Verney brothers' return to the Parliament of March 1553 - a rare feat of brothers being elected to Parliament together as knights of a shire - in which Edmund Verney sat for Buckinghamshire and his brother (probably) for Buckingham, but also Edmund's support of the Duke of Northumberland in the struggle for the royal succession later that year.

These Verneys, besides being young and untried in local administration, were probably seen as troublemakers by those in authority because of their views and associations. The Verney family was distantly related to the Dudley family, who were responsible for trying to put Lady Jane Grey on the English throne instead of the Roman Catholic, Mary Tudor, who was Henry VIII's eldest surviving daughter.

The champion of the Protestant cause, Lady Jane Grey, was married to Lord Guildford Dudley (and the plan was to make her Queen in order to allow John Dudley, the Duke of Northumberland, to exercise as much control over the throne as possible). It seems that Edmund Verney, who was not only related to the Dudleys but was also a staunch Protestant, supported the uprising. Consequently, Mary Tudor, as Queen (1553 – 1558), confined him to his house from 1553 'during the Queen's pleasure'. He also seems to have been fined £100 for supporting the plot to crown Lady Jane Grey as queen.

Yet, together, Edmund and Francis Verney went on to represent Buckinghamshire in 1555, voting with the opposition led by Sir Anthony Kingston and, after the dissolution of the Parliament, they became involved in the

Dudley Conspiracy, of that year. The Dudley Conspiracy, hatched against Queen Mary in December 1555, was so named after one of its main architects, Sir Henry Dudley – a kinsman of John Dudley, the Duke of Northumberland and a relation of the Duke of Suffolk and his daughter, Lady Jane Grey.

In 1553, Sir Henry Dudley had been involved with the attempt to put Lady Jane Grey on the English throne. The Duke of Northumberland had sent Sir Henry to Henri II in France, begging the French King to lead an army into England to support his cause - in return for the surrender of Calais and Guisnes. A few days later, Sir Henry was arrested in Calais and found to have in his possession a great deal of plate and jewellery belonging to the Treasury. Under questioning, he confessed his mission.

Two years later, the rumours that Mary meant to have her absentee husband, Philip of Spain, crowned King of England caused another rebellion. Sir Henry Dudley was one of the prime movers. The idea was to depose Mary and put Henry VIII's other surviving daughter, Elizabeth, on the throne. There were also plans to marry Elizabeth to Edward Courtenay, a distant relative of Edward IV. In December 1555, Sir Henry went to Paris, expecting support from the French King – only to find that Henri II had recently signed a truce with Philip of Spain and so would only give Sir Henry the vaguest of assurances.

Among those questioned about the conspiracy were Edmund and Francis Verney, Henry Peckham (whose sister married a Verney), Lord John Bray, Lord Grey, Lord Thomas Howard, Nicholas Arnold, Nicholas Throckmorton, Sir Peter Killigrew, Sir John Perrot, William Courtenay and Anthony Kingston, who was Comptroller of the Queen's

Household and the Member of Parliament (MP) for Gloucester in the Parliaments of 1545, 1552/ 53 and 1555.

Henry Peckham, the Verneys and Lord Bray were related. The Verneys were MPs. Lord John Bray, their maternal uncle, was the grandson of Sir Reginald Bray, a confidant and minister of Henry VIII and he was Princess Elizabeth's neighbour at Hatfield. Henry Peckham was the younger son of Sir Edward Peckham, brother-in-law of Bray's sister, Mary. Sir Edward Peckham, a knight of Denham, Buckinghamshire, had been Cofferer of the Household to Henry VIII and Treasurer of the Mint under Edward VI and Mary. He held this job under Elizabeth too.

Henry Peckham had been MP for the family borough of Chipping Wycombe (now West Wycombe), Buckinghamshire, in each of Queen Mary's Parliaments until 1555. At first he had been loyal to Queen Mary, as his father had been, and she had awarded him lands in Gloucestershire for his service against the Wyatt Rebellion. He was granted the Manor of Tring in 1555 but, in 1556, he was executed for his part in the plot against Mary.

The date of Edmund Verney's arrest for his part in this plot is not known but he was being interrogated in May 1556 and he was indicted on a charge of treason at Guildhall on 11th June that year. He remained in prison for almost a year and was not pardoned until 12th July 1557.

Edmund Verney died on 13th December 1558 but his burial place is unknown.

He died without leaving either a will or any children but his second wife, Alice, survived him. His affairs were in order at his death for, in February 1554, he had made an indenture with Reginald Bray of Pavenham, Bedfordshire, and Thomas Pigott of Quainton, Buckinghamshire, settling his property 'upon himself and his heirs in tail male'.

However, dying childless, he was succeeded by his third brother, (Sir) Edmund Verney junior.

Thereafter, Pendley seems to have dropped out of the intrigue associated with sixteenth century national politics.

The Verney Room in the modern manor house.

A ghostly Cavalier

The 22 year old Sir Edmund Verney received licence to enter his lands in May 1559, although letters of administration were not granted to John Simpson of Pendley until 17th June 1563. This Sir Edmund Verney (1536 – 1600), who was a captain in the fleet that attacked the Spanish Armada (1588) and was Sheriff of Hertfordshire in 1589, was married three times – first to Frances Hastings, then to Audrey Gardner and finally, to Mary Blakeney. There were two children from these marriages: (Sir) Francis Verney (from Edmund's marriage to Audrey) and (Sir) Edmund Verney (from Edmund's marriage to Mary).

When Sir Edmund died in 1600 - following the Verney tradition - his son and heir, Francis, was a minor. Francis' step-brother, Edmund, was only aged four.

The Verney Room in the modern manor house commemorates the Verney family's Pendley connection.

Before Sir Edmund's death, his third wife, Mary, had persuaded him to divide the inheritance between their son,

Edmund, and her stepson, Francis. This involved the family in getting an Act of Parliament to ratify this arrangement.

The original Pendley Manor house, as it was in the time of Sir Edmund Verney.

When Sir Francis legally came of age, he tried – but failed – to reverse this Act. In the end, he – along with his wife, Ursula, and his step-mother Mary - sold the manor in 1606. Sir Francis, allegedly known to his contemporaries as 'the terror of Hertfordshire', went abroad – and, by all accounts, squandered the money. He became an associate of the pirate captain, Richard Giffard, and died at the Hospital of St Mary of Pity, at Messina, in 1615.

The manor was bought by Sir Richard Anderson, bringing to an end some 150 years of the Verney family's ownership of Pendley. Sir Richard, who became Sheriff of

27

Hertfordshire in 1610, was – in 1631 - fined five shillings for the crime of grazing sheep among his corn.

From a Pendley perspective, it is unfortunate that the manor passed out of the hands of the Verneys when it did. Sir Francis' step-brother, Sir Edmund Verney (1596 – 1642) married Margaret Denton and, although he had misgivings about supporting the Crown in its growing struggle with Parliament's Puritans, he became Knight Marshal and Standard Bearer to King Charles I. He died, aged 46, at the battle of Edgehill, the first pitched battle of the English Civil War. The battle took place in southern Warwickshire – some 57 miles from Pendley – on 23rd October 1642.

Apparently, Sir Edmund's body was never found – but his hand was found, still clutching the Royal Standard. It was identified as his because of the ring, bearing a portrait of King Charles, which it was wearing. At one time, it was said that Sir Edmund's ghost used to haunt Claydon House, a mansion belonging to the Verney family, searching for his lost hand.

Paranormal activity at the current Pendley Manor appears to be confined to the ghost of a young child (who appears to be a little girl) and to a 'lady' who inhabits the first floor of the manor and is noted for always appearing wearing blue slippers. She is said to 'walk' between midnight and two o'clock in the morning.

The child has been seen in the kitchens – notably sitting on top of the dumb waiter - and has also been credited with re-arranging some of the ornaments in the chef's bedroom.

Origin of a President

The Andersons owned Pendley for the next four generations and it was at their house in 1630 that a visitor from Oxford, the Reverend Lawrence Washington (1602 – 1653), the fifth son of Lawrence Washington of Sulgrave Manor, Northamptonshire, encountered a young lady named Amphyllis Twigden. Amphyllis, the daughter and co-heiress of John Twigden of Little Creaton, Northamptonshire, was to bear him six children – the first of whom, John, was illegitimate.

Eventually, this John, as well as his younger siblings, Lawrence and Martha, emigrated to Virginia. John emigrated in 1656 and, on 1st December that year, he married Anne Pope, the daughter of Nathaniel Pope, a gentleman, of Virginia. They had two sons, Lawrence (the grandfather of the first President of the United States of America, George Washington) and John, as well as a daughter, Anne.

The full story is told in the book, 'The Washingtons of Tring', by Murray Neil.

Incidentally, Lawrence Washington's elder brother, Sir William Washington, married Anne Villiers, the half-sister of James I's favourite, George Villiers, 1st Duke of Buckingham.

Meanwhile, the Andersons were still in control of Pendley but, following the death of the last male in the Anderson line, the manor was inherited by his daughter, who had become a Harcourt by marriage. Thus, the manor passed to the Harcourt family.

The parish church in Aldbury contains the burial place of Sir Richard Anderson and his wife, Dame Elizabeth. She was one of the sisters and co-heirs of the Right Honourable George, Lord Viscount Hewitt (also spelled 'Hewyt'), who was Baron of Goran of St Jamestown in Ireland. The church also contains the remains of their two sons, Henry and Richard - who died childless - and their only daughter, Elizabeth, who married Simon Harcourt. Elizabeth and Simon Harcourt had many children but were survived by only two sons, Henry and Richard, and three daughters, Elizabeth, Margaret and Arabella.

The Harcourts traced their ancestry to the Norman Conquest. Simon Harcourt – who married Elizabeth Anderson - was second cousin to Simon, Lord Harcourt, the Lord High Chancellor of England. He was also great nephew to Sir Simon Harcourt, who was Lord Lieutenant of Ireland.

Simon and Elizabeth's son – Henry - married Sarah Frances Bard, the daughter and heiress of Sir John Bard and the Right Honourable the Lady Persiana, who was the daughter of Henry, Earl of Belmore. This was a title, apparently created in 1797 for Armar Lowry-Corry, the first Viscount Belmore, who had previously represented County Tyrone in the Irish House of Commons.

The bodies of all these Harcourts, along with that of Sir Henry's second son, Sir John, are in the church of St John the Baptist, Aldbury.

A new family – and a new Manor House

The last of the Harcourt line at Pendley - Sir William Harcourt – was greatly upset by the loss of fishing when the river Bulbourne was, effectively, destroyed by the building of the Grand Junction Canal in 1800. This led to him leaving Pendley, greatly annoyed with his neighbour, the 4th Earl of Bridgwater, who lived at nearby Ashridge and who was a prime mover in Britain's development of inland waterways.

So, when Pendley's ancient buildings happened to burn down in 1835, William Harcourt wasn't interested in rebuilding the Manor or returning to Pendley.

It was also said that – in absentia – Sir William Harcourt disapproved of the construction of the nearby London and Birmingham Railway, which reached Tring in 1837. According to Arthur MacDonald's 'That Tring Air' *(published in 1944, page 39)*, the 'Comte d'Harcourt' – as William was then styling himself - was living in Paris. A local brewer, John Brown, persuaded William Harcourt's land agent - at the last moment - to sell land for a station and a hotel. This hotel was originally called The Harcourt Arms and, later, The Royal Hotel.

When the railway reached Tring, a new road was built from the station to the town.

According to documents from Wilkins Solicitors, now in the Hertfordshire County Record Office, surveying for the new route started in 1837. This was extremely prompt as the station only opened in October of that year. The surveying continued into 1838. The new road was constructed during 1838 and was certainly complete by 21st September, when two justices of the peace (JPs) inspected it.

The landowners concerned were William Kay (owner of the Tring Park Estate) and the 'Marchioness d'Harcourt' (with one document referring to her as 'Elizabeth Sophia Harcourt, commonly called the Marchioness d'Harcourt').

One document deals with the effect on the Pendley Estate, calculating the footprint of the new road compared with the old road (taking the width of the latter from that set out in the Tring Enclosure Act). The difference was an increase of six poles which, using a land value of £60 per acre, worked out at two pounds and five shillings.

Unfortunately, none of the existing documents have plans attached, although these plans were produced because the bill from the solicitors for drawing them up exists. Without these plans, it is impossible to discover the original route between what is now the junction of Station Road/Grove Road/Cow Lane and where the old and new routes converged - presumably somewhere just west of the canal. There are descriptions, but the names used in the documents are now not recognised. It is likely that the original road went through the Pendley Estate somewhere to the south of the present road. The matter is further complicated by the fact that there were, formerly, different footway and carriage routes, with the footways having a more direct route than the carriageways.

The ruins of the old manor house were removed in 1847 and, in 1864, the estate was auctioned.

It was bought by the Reverend James Williams (1813 - 1871). The diary of Georgiana Williams (James' third daughter and fourth child, who was born in 1850), published in 1997 as 'A Year at Chequers – 1875', states that: 'The Williams family really begins with Joseph Grout, who built up a very successful silk manufacturing business in the early 19th century and came to live at Tring Park in 1844.'

Joseph Grout.

Joseph Grout, who was born in 1776 at Puckeridge, some 30 miles from Tring, was one of five sons of Philip Grout, the village collar maker and saddler.

Apparently, the Grouts – or Growtes – had arrived in Hertfordshire during the 17th century as Protestant

33

fugitives from religious persecution in the Netherlands (where, according to tradition, their surname had been de Groot).

When Joseph Grout's father died in 1794, the collar maker's business couldn't support all of his five sons, so Joseph went to London and found work connected with the silk trade, in Spitalfields. In 1801, he married Elizabeth Clark at St Dunstan's, in Stepney. Theirs was a long but childless marriage.

Joseph's youngest brother, George, joined him in London. Together, they perfected a way of making embossed silk crape – the crape that the fashion of the day prescribed for all forms of mourning. Taking advantage of a plentiful supply of labour – and low wage rates – in East Anglia, they established the firm of Grout & Co in Norwich to throw and weave silk crape.

Over the next ten years, the brothers set up a dyeing and finishing works at Ponders End in Middlesex; moved the crape making factory to larger premises in Norwich; set up new factories in Great Yarmouth and Ditchingham in Norfolk, and opened showrooms in the City of London.

In 1819, they established a silk reeling works in Bhartiparra, near Kolkata, in India. In 1826, the business was worth some £233,000, employed over 3,500 people and was one of the largest crape makers in the country.

Around this time, Joseph Grout moved from Hackney to a large house on Stamford Hill. He remained active in the family firm until shortly before his death in 1852.

His other business interests included being a partner in the East London Waterworks Company and investing in canal companies and coal mines.

Grout & Co received the Royal Warrant in 1895 and, during the Second World War, it was one of only two firms to make parachute silk for the British Government. The company ceased trading in June 1996.

Soon after Grout & Co was established, Joseph had a relationship with a servant, called Sarah Williams. She gave birth to Joseph's son on 24th May 1813, at Mulbarton, near Norwich.

The baby was baptised as 'James Williams'. Obviously, Joseph couldn't marry Sarah but he did pay to educate the boy at Greenwich and Christ's College, Cambridge. In 1838, James took Holy Orders at Ely. It was the same year in which Joseph's wife, Elizabeth, died – at Stamford Hill.

James Grout was a younger brother of Joseph. He had stayed in Puckeridge to carry on the saddler's business. On 12th May 1840, his eldest daughter – Elizabeth – married the Rev James Williams, at Stamford Hill Chapel.

The newly married couple lived with Joseph Grout at his house in Stamford Hill. It was there that their first child was born, in 1843.

James Williams.

The next year, Joseph took the lease for Tring Park (otherwise known as The Mansion). He lived there, with the Rev James Williams, Elizabeth and their growing family, until his death in 1852.

He left his large estate in trust for his grandchildren, with separate life interests to James Williams and Elizabeth Williams.

Elizabeth Williams.

For a short while before his marriage, James Williams appears to have been the curate in the parish of Patteshall, which is in the area of the Grafton Hunt. Subsequently, although many of his friends were clergymen, James doesn't seem to have pursued his vocation actively. Indeed, the 1851 Census records him as a 'clergyman, having no cure of souls'. James fulfilled his obligations to society by being a justice of the peace but occupied the rest of his time with country pursuits – especially hunting and shooting.

37

James, described as being of Glevening Hall in Suffolk, bought the Manor of Pendley at auction in 1864 – and added the neighbouring Manor of Wigginton to his estate in 1868. There is some support for the view that James had hoped to buy the Tring Park Estate but hadn't been able to match the price offered for it by Baron Lionel de Rothschild.

According to the booklet, 'Pendley Residential Centre of Adult Education, the first 25 years, 1945 – 1970' (published in 1970), the passing of the Pendley estate to the Grout/Williams family is recorded thus: '... the Grout family rented Tring Park from the Kay family. In the late (18)60s, the Crown decided to sell Tring Park. The Grouts, at about this time changing their name to Williams... were interested and made an offer. A bigger offer was made by the Rothschilds, who already owned Waddesdon, Mentmore, Ascott, Halton and Aston Clinton.

'The townspeople, in a touching exhibition of loyalty, tried to raise money to bridge the gap between the offer of the Williams' and that of the Rothschilds. The £600 they raised was scarcely sufficient and Tring Park passed to the Rothschilds. Lord Rothschild, a sensitive as well as a most charitable man, sensed the local feeling and sold off to the Rev James Williams at a very reasonable price the old Pendley estate.'

However there seem to be a few inconsistencies about this rather romantic story. For those who care for such things as facts and the truth, it's important to outline these. It's time for some chronology:

1679 The Tring Park Estate ceases to be Crown property. From then on, its ownership was in private hands. It was owned first by Henry Guy; then by four generations of the Gore family, followed by Sir Drummond Smith.

1823 William Kay buys the Tring Park Estate from the Executors of Sir Drummond Smith. William Kay didn't live in The Mansion. He let it out.

1838 Kay died and was succeeded by his youngest son – who, with impressive unoriginality, was also called William. William Kay senior's will contained complicated provisions for the future ownership of the Tring Park Estate should William Kay junior not have children - which he didn't.

1844 Joseph Grout rents The Mansion from William Kay. Almost certainly, both men knew each other through their connections with the silk trade.

1857 There was a dispute over the future ownership of the estate – set out in William Kay senior's will. This resulted in the affairs of the Tring Park Estate being taken over by the Court of Chancery. Incidentally, James Williams and his family were still living in The Mansion.

1864 James Williams bought the Pendley estate from the Harcourts.

1865 William Kay junior died.

1871 James Williams died.

1872 The Court of Chancery sells the Tring Park Estate at auction. It was bought by Baron (an Austrian title) Lionel de Rothschild. Although he now owned the Estate, Lionel Rothschild did not live there. The Williams family moved to Chequers while the new Pendley manor house was built.

1874 Nathaniel Rothschild took up residence at Tring Park.

1877 JG Williams moved in to the new manor house at Pendley.

1879 Lionel de Rothschild died.

1885 Nathaniel Rothschild is made the (1st) Lord Rothschild.

So, there appears to be some truth in the story that James Williams wanted to buy the Tring Park Estate in 1872 - and, since he didn't buy it, couldn't afford it. However, at no point was Pendley part of the Tring Park Estate. Moreover, James Williams had owned Pendley since 1864 – so he couldn't have bought it again, in 1872, from a man who had never owned it.

This book has already explored the truth behind the delightfully vague phrase, 'The Grouts, at about this time changing their name to Williams...'

James Williams began planning a new manor house at Pendley – in 1870 - but died (in 1871) before the work could be started. His wife, Elizabeth, only survived him by a year. They are both buried in the family vault at Aldbury parish church.

So, at the age of 24, James and Elizabeth's eldest son, Joseph Grout Williams – known as 'JG' – inherited the largest part of the family estate; with his brothers and sisters receiving legacies. At the time, they were still living at Tring Park.

Joseph Grout Williams.

In those days, the new manor house at Pendley was no more than a set of plans, so the family rented Chequers –

which, in 1921, became the country house retreat of Britain's Prime Ministers – until the new Pendley Manor was habitable. The new house at Pendley took five years to build and the Williams family moved into the new manor house in 1877.

JG commissioned the London-based Scottish architect, Walter Fitzgerald Knox Lyon (1844 – 1894), to build a new Tudor style manor house at Pendley. It was designed to reflect the interests of the Williams family – especially those of 'JG', who was a keen agriculturalist and horticulturalist. Apparently, according to a contemporary account, the new manor house was 'built a short distance above the site of the old manor house' and 'was intended to give the idea of an old English hall, added to at different periods'.

The new manor house commissioned by Joseph Grout Williams.

The grounds were laid out by a Mr Marnock. It was said that only the new stables, with its courtyard, in any way resembled the original Pendley Manor, which had been largely rebuilt by Sir Richard Anderson in the seventeenth century.

The Drawing Room as it was in 1894. The room is now used as the Restaurant.

The other end of the Drawing Room at Pendley Manor - now used as the Restaurant.

The room some 125 years later.

The other end of the room some 125 years later.

Born in 1848, JG was educated at Harrow and at Trinity College Cambridge. Contemporary accounts record him as being small and 'rather delicate' but 'quite a tough character and a keen sportsman, who often hunted six days a week'.

JG was a successful breeder of Shire horses, pedigree cattle and Hampshire downs sheep. He was also one of the chief supporters of the Tring Show – which was held in the grounds of Tring Park up until the beginning of the Second World War. Subsequently, it was merged with other local shows around the county to form the Herts Show.

JG was also a captain in the Buckinghamshire Yeomanry, a Justice of the Peace, and was High Sheriff of Hertfordshire in 1889 (becoming not only the first owner of Pendley to be the county's High Sheriff since Sir Richard Anderson, 279 years previously but also becoming the manor's last High Sheriff).

45

Sheep Sale at Pendley. July 29ᵗʰ 1907.

Frank Brown and Donald Brown conduct a sale of JG Williams' Hampshire Downs sheep at Pendley on 29th July 1907. That year, JG had had considerable success at the Northampton and Peterborough Shows and the resulting sheep sale attracted a great deal of interest. The average price achieved for the animals was £7 – 17 – 6d, which was a considerable sum in those days. JG's Hampshire Downs sheep were in the care of Mr H Best, who is described as an 'expert shepherd'.

Haymaking at Pendley.

JG took seriously his responsibilities within the local community. Not only did he give the land for the erection of St Cross Church in the nearby village of Wilstone, in 1877, but he donated a large sum of money towards the cost of the building. He was also responsible for providing that village - in 1875 - with a small hall and caretaker's cottage, first named 'The British Workman's Temperance Room', which stood between the Buckingham Arms Public House and the Village Stores.

In 1878 – the year after the new Pendley Manor was completed, he married Catherine Mary Tidswell, daughter of Robert Tidswell (who had been a partner in Grout & Co's crape manufacturing business from 1840 until his death in 1856). The Tidswell and Grout/ Williams families had been friendly for more than 30 years by the time that JG married Catherine (who was known as Katie).

Pendley Manor in 1880. Photograph reproduced by permission.

The front of Pendley Manor, photographed c 1890. Photograph reproduced by permission.

The back of Pendley Manor including the gardens, photographed before the First World War. Photograph reproduced by permission.

Pendley Manor in 1911. Photograph reproduced by permission.

Staff at Pendley Manor, photographed on 19th September 1888.
Pictured are: (back row, from left) S. Butcher, John Clement (butler), F.
Sturman, Henry Beer. (front row, from left) Mrs Vock, with 'Glen', Mary
Anne Wells, with 'Gip', and Emma. Photograph reproduced by
permission.

Tring Cyclists' Club members visit Pendley Manor, 1898. Photograph
reproduced by permission.

JG and Katie didn't have any children. JG died on 9th October
1923, aged 75 – and his coffin was taken to Aldbury for his
funeral, on 13th October, on one of his own carts drawn by
his Shire horses. Simultaneously with the funeral in
Aldbury, a memorial service to JG was held at Tring parish
church, where JG had been a churchwarden for some 40
years.

Joseph Grout Williams' funeral.

The last Williams at Pendley

The estate then passed to JG and Katie's nephew, Vivian Dunbar Stanley Williams. He didn't move to Tring because he lived at Greens Norton, from where he was Master of the Grafton Hunt. However, JG's widow, Katie, continued to live at Pendley – in some style - until her death in 1944. Up until the Second World War, Pendley employed 11 gardeners, a butler, two footmen, along with coachmen, houseboys and the rest of the retinue that a country house was expected to have in the late 19th and early 20th centuries.

Recalling those days, the estate's last private owner, Dorian Williams, reminisced – in his book 'Pendley and a Pack of Hounds': 'The style of it all! Family prayers, tennis parties, 'treats' in the housekeeper's room (considerably more suited to young people's appetites than four formal but inadequate courses in the great dining room), carriages in the stable, the old station coach which used to be taken up to the ring-side for Tring Show, a walk round the shrubberies with a gun in the evening, accompanied by old Puddephat, the keeper, whose father had been murdered by poachers in the 1860s, 'cherry pie' and geraniums round the sundial and the dogs' cemetery in the rockery.

'It's no good pretending that, as children, we loved Pendley when we went there for holiday visits… As one grew up, however, one appreciated it more. By the time war came in 1939, it seemed somehow to stand for the past. Our past in particular as, by then, we'd left our own home in Northamptonshire – my mother being driven by a hunting accident to the sun and, after three years abroad, to Somerset, which was never really home to us now working in London.'

51

How Dorian Williams (JG and Katie's great-nephew) came to inherit Pendley is quite complex.

JG's sister, Frances (known as Fanny) was born in 1846 and became Mrs Robin Craufurd on 18th July 1872. Fanny and 'Robin' were married for four years before Fanny's health gave out and she died. Her husband – Henry Robert Gregan Craufurd, who was known as 'Robin' – had been born in Italy. He was a 'gentleman of independent means' and, among other things, was a Justice of the Peace.

In 1878, Robin Craufurd married again. This time, he married Alice Jane Wood, the eldest daughter of the Rector of Aldbury (since 1862), the Rev Richard Mountford Wood – whose family claimed indirect descent from Josiah Wedgwood (1730 – 1795), the prominent slavery abolitionist and the founder of the pottery company that still bears his name.

Alice's brother, Henry took Holy Orders and followed his father as Rector of Aldbury. In 1911, Henry's daughter, Violet May Thellusson Wood, married Vivian Dunbar Stanley Williams, whose father was George Stanley Williams – a brother of JG.

George Stanley (known as Stanley) was born in 1852 and followed JG to Harrow. Leaving Harrow, he attended Sandhurst and was commissioned in the 8th Hussars in 1873. In 1878, Stanley saw action with his regiment on the Khyber Pass during the Second Afghan War and was promoted to the rank of captain.

The wedding reception at Pendley Manor. July 31. 1907

The reception at Pendley Manor on 31st July 1907 following the wedding of Ivy Elizabeth Marion Williams, the eldest child of JG Williams' younger brother, the late Captain Stanley Williams of the 8th Hussars. The groom was Arthur Thomas Crawford Cree, the eldest son of Arthur W Cree, of Brockworth, Beckenham. The wedding service was performed by the Rev ED Cree, the groom's great uncle, and the Rev TG Cree, the groom's uncle, aided by Tring's vicar, the Rev H Francis. At the time of his marriage, Arthur was a barrister. He died – killed in action - in Belgium on 12th May 1915. At that time, he was a lieutenant in The Durham Light Infantry. Ivy did not re-marry and died in 1981, aged 98.

Ivy and Arthur had three children: Elizabeth, Janet and Eleanor. Elizabeth is the mother of Robin Knox-Johnston, the round-the-world yachtsman.

His military career was ended when he was cited – by his colonel – in a divorce suit. Stanley and his new partner, Mrs Adelaide Foster (née Manders) – formerly the colonel's wife - returned to England and married as soon as the law allowed. However, as a divorced woman, Adelaide was never really 'accepted' at Pendley. So Stanley and Adelaide went to live in Leicestershire, renting Kirkby Hall near

Atherstone. Over the following ten years they hunted regularly with the Atherstone and the Quorn Hunts, and also found time to have five children.

From the wedding of Vivian Williams and Violet Mary Thellusson Wood, 1st February 1911. The service was held at Aldbury parish church where Miss Wood's father was the rector, and the reception was held at Pendley Manor. The two young attendants are Mary Cree, the bride's niece, and Jack Finch, the bride's cousin. The bridesmaids are (from left) Beryl Hawtrey, Miss Craufurd and Katie Finch (all cousins of the bride), Aline Tidswell, Miss Kenney and Gillian Bloxam. The best man is EJ Nettlefold who, along with the bridegroom, was a member of the 5th Dragoon Guards.

In 1890, JG bought an Elizabethan manor house – Brooksby Hall, near Melton Mowbray - in the heart of Quorn country for Stanley, Adelaide and their family. After three years, Stanley and Adelaide's money ran out. Stanley took the children to a smaller house nearby, while Adelaide obtained a separation agreement and left. Stanley then discovered that Adelaide had had a lover in Brooksby; so he divorced her.

Three generations of Williams' at Pendley: JG (standing), Ivy Cree (née Williams) (sitting) with her first two children: Elizabeth (standing) and Janet, who was born on 10th March 1910 and baptised on 20th April 1910, at Aldbury, by the Rector of Albury, the Rev HT Wood (the father of Violet Mary Thellusson Wood, who was to marry Vivian Williams in 1911).

Stanley died a year later, following a fall while out hunting. The children were taken to Pendley to be brought up by JG and Katie – and all memories of Adelaide were expunged as far as was possible.

Adelaide died about 1930, 'somewhere on the South Coast' but, by the time of the marriage of her second son, Vivian Dunbar Stanley Williams, to Violet May Thellusson Wood in 1911, Adelaide had spent some time in prison for fraud.

It was the marriage of Vivian Williams and Violet Wood – on 1st February 1911 - that produced Dorian Williams (July 1914 – July 1985). Dorian lived at and, later, inherited Pendley - although, during World War II, some two thirds of the house were used by the Women's Land Army as a hostel.

An aerial view of Pendley, taken probably between the Wars. The picture is looking at the back of the property. The road on the left is Station Road and the properties in the foreground are now private houses. At the time of publication, it is still possible to see the wall to the walled garden.

Violet Williams (nee Wood) was an accomplished – and prize-winning – horsewoman. After she died, in 1944, Vivian married again. His second wife, Brenda, also shared his passion for horses. She trained horses and was a member of the Great Britain dressage team that competed in the Stockholm (1956) and Rome (1960) Olympics.

Violet Williams, Dorian's mother.

Dorian Williams was a British equestrian, journalist, broadcaster, author and patron of the arts. Educated at

Hawtreys Preparatory School and Harrow School, he became - for over 35 years from 1949 - the voice of show jumping on British television. In 1938, he had married the Honourable Moyra Lubbock (1918 – 1992), the daughter of Lord Avebury, but the marriage was dissolved in 1949 – the year that he founded the Pendley Open Air Shakespeare Festival in the grounds of Pendley Manor and became BBC television's voice of show jumping. In 1956, Dorian married for a second time: Jennifer (Neale), who collaborated with him on a number of his publications, as illustrator and editor.

Dorian Williams.

Pendley Manor, on Dorian and Jennifer Williams' wedding day, 1956.
Photograph reproduced by permission.

Dorian Williams was largely responsible for turning show jumping into a mainstream television sport. His last broadcast was in 1985, a few months before he died, of cancer, aged 71.

Dorian Williams was a writer as well as a commentator. He wrote the 'Wendy' series of 'traditional pony books' for children, along with two adult 'horse novels', 'Pancho' and 'Kingdom for a Horse'. He also wrote several non-fiction works, concerning equestrianism and, especially, show jumping.

He was Master of the Whaddon Chase hunt (from 1954 to 1980) as well as Chairman of the British Horse Society, and was instrumental in setting up the National Equestrian Centre at Stoneleigh Abbey in Warwickshire. In 2005, he was one of the inaugural laureates appointed to The British Horse Society Equestrian Hall of Fame.

A Residential Centre of Adult Education

With the return of peace after the end of the Second World War, Dorian Williams established the Manor as what was then a revolutionary new type of Adult Education Centre.

In his book, 'Pendley and a Pack of Hounds' (published in 1959), Dorian Williams attributed the beginnings of the idea for the Centre to 3rd February 1944. Apparently, Dorian had been 'laid up for some months with a bad leg'. It had given him time to think. He wrote: 'While running an evacuated boys' school in Wales during the early years of the war, I had found myself quite unexpectedly connected at first hand with education for adults. Throwing open the school during the holidays for all and sundry – service people, men and women from industry, people of all ages confined to London and other cities and months of bombing – it soon became apparent that something must be laid on for the inmates if bad weather, lack of transport and limitation of amenities were not to lead to boredom. Accordingly various activities were arranged such as lectures, films, discussion groups, play readings, music recitals and, of course, talks by anyone who had an interesting story to tell... Later in the war, experience with the service educational activities and practical work in the educational field confirmed these findings.'

Later in the book, he describes visiting Pendley one Sunday afternoon in early May 1945, after being in London: 'Pendley was at one of its bests – the other best is in October. There was lilac in every shrubbery, a profusion of blossom of every hue, from deep red to snowy white. A few defiant daffodils still lorded it on the bank and up the glade. The heady scent of wallflowers wafted up to me from the border below the library veranda where I sat drinking it all in. The soothing cooing of the wood pigeons made a drowsy background and even the raucous caw-cawing of rooks and restless drumming of woodpeckers from the great belt of cedars, chestnut and beech screening the garden from the west, sounded contentedly harmonious. Already the sun was slanting, throwing great shadows across the lawn and, by the strength of its glow behind the trees, making a fretsaw pattern of branches, twigs and early leaf.

'The peace was absolute and one revelled in it absolutely. A few hours before [in London], I had been tired, jaded, despondent. A few miles away there was noise, clamour – even bombs. And here was peace and beauty – and calm. Suddenly one felt relaxed and whole; no longer torn to shreds by the shattering pace and turmoil of life in a twentieth century city.

'Now I knew what Pendley had to do. If Pendley could do this for me in a few brief hours on a Sunday afternoon, then how much more might it not do it to the thousands who lived and worked all their lives in the congested, baffling cities, who had never known Pendley before; who had seldom even known the country? Such an experience, however short it might be, could only be beneficial.'

This is, of course, a sentiment that many (including Pendley's current owners, no doubt) would endorse. Dorian came to the conclusion that 'the tired, perhaps disturbed, mind – after months and years in factories and overcrowded offices' would be helped by a few hours of peace, calm and beauty, after which the mind would become receptive to new knowledge.

Above is the hallway staircase at Pendley Manor in about the late
1940s. Photograph reproduced by permission. Below is the hallway
some 70 years later.

After discussion with the education authorities, including John Newsom and Douglas Cooke, the education officers for Hertfordshire and Buckinghamshire respectively, Dorian and two friends, Roger Pulbrook and Kenneth Bowden, began planning a series of weekend courses in drama, music, natural history, philosophy, art, archaeology, religion and Shakespeare. The only snags were that they had no money and, more importantly at the time, the Women's Land Army was still in possession of Pendley.

Pendley was de-requisitioned on 1st July 1945 and the Pendley Residential Centre for Adult Education – the first of its kind in the country – was opened on 31st October of the same year.

Pendley Manor in 1945. Photograph reproduced by permission.

From March 1946, the Centre began operating seven days a week, offering a varied lecture programme as well as non-vocational courses.

Three firms - Vauxhall Motors, Carreras and Cadburys – took the unusual step (at the time) of agreeing to send their employees to these courses *and* to pay those employees' wages while they were on the courses. In addition, the paper manufacturers, Wiggins Teape, had a timber sectional building on their own land which is now part of Pendley Manor's car park. There are no specific records to hand about whether their employees were enrolled onto courses at Pendley but it seems reasonable to believe that they were.

Around 1947, an article published in *Personnel Management and Welfare* said that: 'reports from Vauxhall Motors, whose employees had attended mid-week cultural courses at Pendley Manor, stated that those attending were more responsive to reasoned argument, more alive, better adjusted to the group in which they worked and, generally, improved in their attitude to their job. Whether or not this is true in all cases, it could be anticipated that employers would benefit in the long run by an all-round improvement of their employees.'

An example of the Adult Education Centre's programme – taken from 1947 – is:

FRIDAY, 15th AUGUST

7 pm   PLASTICS, practical Class

8 pm   Opening session of weekend course THE
                 ENGLISH WAY

                 PAGES FROM THE PAST, The Stuarts – The
                 Pendley Staff

SATURDAY, 16th AUGUST

9.45 am	THE ENGLISH FARM, a conducted tour

5 pm	ENGLISH ART – Patric Stevenson

8 pm	PAGES FROM THE PAST, The Elizabethans

SUNDAY, 17th AUGUST

2.30 pm	THE ENGLISH LANGUAGE – Dorian Williams

5 pm	PAGES FROM THE PAST, The Tudors

8 pm	ENGLISH MUSIC – Patric Stevenson

TUESDAY, 19th AUGUST

2.45 pm	WOMEN'S AFTERNOON – Music followed by Talk and Screen Competition – Roger Pilkington

THURSDAY, 21st AUGUST

EVERYONE CAN ENJOY GOOD MUSIC

7 pm	A Music for Middlebrows: Miscellaneous Records – Dorian Williams
	B Musical Analysis – Patric Stevenson

8 pm	BEETHOVEN's SYMPHONY No. 1 – First in a series of Beethoven's nine symphonies

FRIDAY, 22nd AUGUST

7 pm	PLASTICS, practical Class

8 pm	Opening session of weekend course "ENGLISH SOCIAL HISTORY - 18th and 19th centuries

Admission to Lectures - Evenings 6d, Weekends 1s.

Among the many stories told about the Centre in Dorian Williams' book, 'Pendley and a Pack of Hounds' is: 'A somewhat unfortunate incident occurred when three elderly ladies, visiting Pendley for the first time, for a winter weekend, elected to go for a walk in the grounds after the first evening lecture. As they had never been to Pendley before and had arrived when it was already dark and foggy, this was a little rash.

'Not surprisingly, coming to a sharp turn in a garden path where it comes up to the ha-ha, they failed to see the corner and all pitched over the sunk-fence. Worse, they got themselves suspended upside down on the barbed wire strand set out from the ha-ha to prevent the cattle climbing up from the park. Fortunately, taking my dog for a run before going to bed, I came across the unhappy sight which, in the almost total darkness, resembled three outsize black crows hung up, as they are by gamekeepers, as a warning to other vermin.

'With the help of my secretary they were released and, covered in blood, their clothes torn, they were helped inside and hurried into a bath. This, in future, was known as the night of the blood-baths.

'One of the ladies later became a Pendley "regular". The other two we never heard of again!'

Christmas at Pendley

'An ideal setting for Christmas with its panelling, its great open fires, its Victorian atmosphere... and a fireside reading round a great log fire in the panelled hall.'

During these years, when it came to Christmas, the Centre offered its customers an 'old fashioned Christmas', reserving a number of places for people from overseas who would, otherwise, in all probability, have been on their own for Christmas. According to Dorian Williams, 'Originally we had advertised our Christmas at Pendley "for those who would otherwise be on their own" but, after a few hours of the first Christmas, we realised only too clearly why they would have been on their own! Subsequently, we encouraged people of every sort and every age.

'Pendley is an ideal setting for Christmas with its panelling, its great open fires, its Victorian atmosphere. Christmas Eve, when we have a fireside reading round a great log fire in the panelled hall, with nothing but candlelight and holly and the great kissing bough hanging from the central chandelier is unforgettable – especially when, at the end, carollers or hand-bell ringers entertain from the gallery.

'There are always a number of guests from other countries and, on the occasion to which I refer, after lunch on Christmas day, while waiting for the Queen's Speech – or the King's, as it then was – we invited all from abroad to tell us, briefly, of "Christmas in my land".

'Eventually it was the turn of an African.

'He rose slowly, humbly and stood for a moment, bashful and silent. He was magnificent to look at – well over six feet. He smiled. His teeth were very white and his eyes twinkled. He fingered his little moustache.

'"How shall I say this?" he started.

'"You see, Christianity is something quite new to me and to my country. My father was the first man in our land ever to hear of Jesus Christ. He was fifty when he heard of him and he was very thrilled. He was still very thrilled when I was old enough for him to tell me about Jesus, only a few years ago. And now *I* am very thrilled – still very thrilled. But you perhaps are not so thrilled any more. You have known of Jesus for more than a thousand years and, perhaps, you take him now for granted. But in my land, he is new. For us, he is alive."

'And he sat down. He was Seretse Khama, the young King of Bechuanaland. Sitting by his side was a girl called Ruth. They had just met. His faith in Jesus supported him, I hope, in the troubles he was so soon to face.

'It seemed worth it, that Christmas, to have opened Pendley and gone through all that it entailed, just to have had the experience of listening to that fine African's simple statement of faith.

'It made one humble. It made one think. Wasn't that what Pendley was for?'

A new regime – and characters

Pendley Manor's college teaching staff relax.

The Manor's 'college period' was run by a colourful group of characters. Murray Fieldhouse ran the pottery courses. He arrived at Pendley during his demob (de-mobilisation) leave from the RAF, enjoyed the Pendley experience and asked if there was a job available. Dorian Williams replied – jokingly – that the only job available was 'washer-up' in the pantry. Murray agreed to do the job, providing he could indulge his spare time in doing some pottery. During his time at Pendley, Murray built up a nationwide reputation as a potter and his pottery courses were much sought-after.

Stuart Ready was a retired actor who taught English to the so-called 'au pairs' – who were mainly German girls and who were, effectively, unpaid skivvies at the Manor. In addition, other long-term regulars at Pendley included Mrs

Moffatt, the 'gammy-legged cook'; 'Pepe', the barman; John Hollifield and Ron Allsopp, who were successive bursars.

Ronnie Evers was the warden at Pendley Manor for many years. He had been Headmaster of Berkhamsted School when Dorian Williams recruited him to play comedy leads in the Pendley Shakespeare Festival – more of which later. Ronnie and his wife, Marjorie, who was also heavily involved in the annual Shakespeare Festival, lived on-site in a house – called Paddock House - near the stable block.

Within three years, the Centre attracted over 3,000 customers a year. By 1950 these numbers had increased steadily. Over 40 per cent of the Centre's students came from industry, sent to Pendley by their employers. Over 100 firms now sent their employees to Pendley in this way. However, costs were also rising steadily and the Centre was only just breaking even.

Dorian Williams (right) watches Murray Fieldhouse (centre) with a student on a pottery course at Pendley. Photograph reproduced by permission.

The attendance figures in 1970 – some 25 years after the Centre began – were: 2,500 courses, attended by 100,000 people. This figure includes 7,000 foremen / supervisors from 250 firms attending over 300 courses. In addition, the annual Shakespeare Festival attracted audiences of 10,000 people a year by 1970.

However, over 20 similar centres of adult education – all following the Pendley model – had been opened around the country by 1950. This number had increased to 30 by 1970. These centres included Attingham Park in Shropshire, Burton Manor on the Wirral, Missenden Abbey in Buckinghamshire, Knuston Hall in Northamptonshire, Urchfont Manor in Wiltshire, Grantley Hall in Yorkshire, Dillington House in Somerset, Belstead House in Suffolk, Barlaston Hall in Staffordshire and Wansfell in Essex.

Murray Fieldhouse demonstrating pottery - on camera - at Pendley.

Pendley students watch a pottery demonstration by Murray Fieldhouse, held in the conservatory at Pendley.

In 1950, Dorian Williams brought the BBC's television cameras to Pendley to film a programme on fox hunting. Photograph reproduced by permission.

Like many others in those days, Jose Antonio Lopez – popularly known as Pepe - the barman (and general helper) at Pendley from 1964 to 1987, came to Pendley to improve his English language skills. According to Pepe, most of the staff in those days were from countries including Germany, Switzerland, the Netherlands, Sweden, France, Spain and Yugoslavia.

Jose Antonio Lopez – popularly known as Pepe - the barman at Pendley for over 20 years.

On his own admission, he stayed at Pendley because the whole community there was a family. It felt like – and became – home to all those connected with it.

"We ate the same things that the clients ate – and, every day at 4pm in the Manor's hall, there was coffee and tea, with homemade sandwiches and cakes," he said.

"Every Monday to Friday, Pendley was host to conferences, with the weekends being given over mainly to pleasure. In those days, Pendley was a venue for large parties – of between 200 and 400 guests. In addition to Police Balls, Football and Rugby Club events, The Pony Club and various charities held prestigious events there. Of course, there was the annual Hunt Ball, since Dorian Williams was Master of the Whaddon Chase hunt and an extremely keen equestrian.

"For such events, we had one bar in the conservatory and another downstairs," he said. The downstairs bar was sited where the sauna and steam rooms are now.

"The annual open air Shakespeare Festival was always a big event," Pepe continued. "For me, it involved running a bar for the public, who came to see the plays, and another for the house's residents. On the last night of the Festival, there used to be two performances – one from 7pm to 10pm and the other from 11pm to 1am – and it used to be a difficult but well organised manoeuvre to get the first audience out while the second audience arrived, without the two audiences meeting and causing traffic chaos on the roads bordering the estate.

"Pendley was in demand at other times of the year, too," he added. "Easter week attracted amateur painters to the Manor but there were weekends devoted to Scottish dancing, meditation, Japanese flower arrangement and folk music, among other things."

Pendley attracted film companies too. Some scenes in the 1983 film, 'Princess Daisy' were shot at Pendley – bringing Claudia Cardinale, among others, to the house. Part of the TV mini-series, 'The Far Pavilions' (1984) was also shot at Pendley.

"In addition to Claudia Cardinale, I met a lot of well-known celebrities at Pendley over the years," said Pepe. "There were show jumping celebrities, of course, including Her Royal Highness Princess Anne, the Princess Royal, but there were politicians too – such as Michael Foot and Sir Geoffrey Howe – along with the American business magnate, Nubar Gulbenkian, and even the comedian, Dave Allen."

Francina Duyker arrived from Holland to work at Pendley in February 1953. Her account of her time there – told in the booklet 'Pendley Residential Centre of Adult Education, the first 25 years, 1945 – 1970' (published in 1970) – echoes Pepe's view. Francina wrote: 'Arriving at Pendley I was very impressed: the long winding drive, the beautiful trees, the lovely green lawns and, most of all, the splendid old mansion itself...

'The next day I was introduced to the staff – people of all walks of life – amongst them several girls, like myself, from the Continent. We formed a good team. Whatever needed doing was done by whoever was available, from making beds and tending the lawns to feeding the hound puppies.

'The most delightful thing about Pendley in those days was the splendid social life we had. We freely mingled with the guests and were at liberty to participate in all the activities that were going on and, with so many courses being conducted, it was not hard to find something of interest.

'Of course, the chores had to be done first. We challenged each other by increasing the number of beds we could make, the speed with which we could do the dusting, the washing up and the preparation of sandwiches.

'Very often, on Mondays, when there were no new guests yet, we had a staff dinner, usually presided over by the Lord of the Manor himself – an occasion which most girls were looking forward to because Dorian had no difficulty in keeping them spellbound by all the marvellous stories he had to tell.'

Francina – who became Francina Ewell – rose to become housekeeper at Pendley before going on to work for the London County Council as Matron at several of its residential schools. Later, she worked for the Greater London Council, at County Hall in London.

Up to now

Towards the end of his time at Pendley – and, indeed, his life - Dorian Williams created a sports complex off Cow Lane, Tring, which is close to Pendley Manor. This sports complex contains pitches and clubhouses for football, rugby, squash and bowls. In addition, he oversaw the conversion of the indoor riding school into a theatre in 1975. Originally, what is now the Court Theatre was an indoor tennis court but, later, it became an indoor riding school before being purely used for storage.

The indoor riding school at Pendley.

Many people in Tring would count all of these facilities as the most enduring parts of Dorian Williams' legacy to the community.

After Dorian Williams' death in 1985, the Pendley estate was bought by The Grass Roots Group (GRG). Its owner, David Evans, found the house too impractical to use as offices and, instead, converted the stable block and then sold the Manor on to become a hotel. Currently, GRG still owns the stables - which are known as 'Pennyroyal Court' - and the Court Theatre, which is heavily used by the local community.

In 1987, Pendley Manor was bought – for £1.2m - by an independent hotelier and entrepreneur, Vinu Bhattessa. A native of Kenya, Vinu was attracted to Pendley not only by the 'look and feel' of the house but also by the annual Shakespeare Festival – which was taking place during his first encounter with Pendley.

His introduction to Pendley Manor as a prospective buyer, a little later that year, was oddly reminiscent, in a way, of the infamous 'night of the blood-baths' (see: 'A Residential Centre of Adult Education').

Unsure of what to expect, Vinu Bhattessa decided to drive to Pendley from Central London, one cold, wet autumn evening, to inspect the Manor house.

Rather like those unfortunate three ladies of many years previously, the visit didn't begin well. About 50 metres along the hotel driveway from Cow Lane, while dodging potholes, Vinu's car got stuck in the mud.

There were no lights. Mobile phones were in their infancy. Disconcerted but undeterred, Vinu knocked on the door of 'The Lodge' at the entrance to the Manor's grounds and asked for help. The Lodge's owner kindly called for a tow truck to help get Vinu's car out of the mud.

Two hours later, Vinu managed to complete his journey – driving the final few metres to the front of the Manor house.

At that time, the house was largely derelict. Visitors, such as Vinu – who, on that first autumnal visit, was clutching a torch and wondering what there was to discover in this decaying yet intriguing building - were required to wear hard hats on entering the house. Indeed, at that time, the grand hall staircase was unsafe to climb.

Vinu was surprised that the manor had fallen into such a state of disrepair. Nonetheless – as with so many other people over the years – for Vinu, Pendley was a case of love at first sight.

Before beginning that evening's drive back to London, Vinu had decided that he was going to reinstate the Manor house to its former glory. Over the next five years, he did exactly that.

In 1987, when Vinu Bhattessa bought the Manor, the house had 38 bedrooms and just two bathrooms. By 1989, it had been restored and it re-opened as a country house hotel. At that stage, 24 bedrooms and 24 bathrooms had been added to the house. The following year, a further 53 bedrooms were added.

Then, in May 1991, the addition of the Harcourt ballroom, banqueting room and meeting rooms, together with its 73 modern bedrooms, as well as a swimming complex, turned Pendley Manor into a country house conference and event venue. The official opening of this phase of Pendley's development was carried out by the Rt Hon Kenneth Baker MP – who was, at the time, the Home Secretary.

The Harcourt ballroom....

... and meeting rooms.

The restoration and continued development of Pendley Manor became, and has remained, an important project for Vinu. Despite his many other achievements in the UK and around the world, Vinu is proudest of his achievements at

Pendley - and he views Pendley Manor as much more than 'just a business'.

The Rt Hon Kenneth Baker MP opens Pendley Manor's new phase of development in 1991. Sudha and Vinu Bhattessa are pictured with him on the far left and far right of the picture, respectively.

Similar degrees of commitment and loyalty are also evident among Pendley's staff – a number of whom have been working at the hotel since its re-opening in 1989.

Pendley has become such an integral part of Vinu's and his family's life that it was the venue for his eldest daughter's marriage. Over the years, Vinu's three children - and now his grandchildren - have all celebrated their key birthdays there. Moreover, it's where Vinu and his wife, Sudha, celebrated their 40th wedding anniversary.

Since he bought Pendley in the late 1980s, Vinu has developed an intimate knowledge of the Manor – but the Manor continues to provide occasional surprises for him.

His first intriguing discovery came in 1988, while the building was being restored. At that time, he asked why did extendable brass rails surround the fireplace in the Shakespeare Bar? The answer was that they were designed to hold newspapers, so that any wet ink on the newspapers could dry in front of the fire before the papers were read. The fireplace and the rails remain, although the ink on today's newspapers always arrives dry.

More recently, some refurbishment work carried out in 2010 led to the discovery of the Manor house's original parquet wooden floors. They had been well preserved under layers of carpet. After six months of meticulous restoration, the floors in the Great Hall, the Shakespeare Bar, the Verney Room and the Restaurant were unveiled to the public and can still be seen in their full glory today.

The results of Vinu's efforts at Pendley have also borne fruit in wider contexts. Apart from restoring the Manor and, so, making available once again to the local community a part of its heritage, the Manor offers that community enhanced sporting and social facilities. For lovers of the performing arts – and, indeed, picnics - there is also the annual Shakespeare Festival (see 'Pendley's Shakespeare connection' and 'Appendix: A personal perspective of Pendley'). This Festival, begun in 1949 has continued to run since Vinu Bhattessa bought Pendley Manor - except for 1988, when major construction work on the house was underway and health and safety issues forced the cancellation of that year's productions.

Interestingly, Vinu's involvement in the Pendley Shakespeare Festival led him to becoming a donor to help the reconstruction of The Globe Theatre, in London.

More recently – at the suggestion of David Evans, of GRG - Vinu has been delighted to contribute to Chilfest, an event which takes place on the Pendley meadows and supports local charities.

Pendley Manor's owner for over 25 years, Vinu Bhattessa, introduced its now iconic peacocks to the Manor's grounds.

It was Vinu Bhattessa who introduced peacocks to Pendley. Apparently, one of the plays in Pendley's Shakespeare Festival required a couple of peacocks – to add some further colour to the proceedings. So Vinu provided a pair. After the festival, they stayed – and soon there were around

85

50 of them. Subsequently, their numbers have been controlled and the current crop of Pendley peacocks and peahens numbers around ten.

Afternoon tea in the Peacock Lounge at Pendley Manor Hotel and Conference Centre.

Pendley's Shakespeare connection

Dorian Williams was a keen amateur actor who, in 1949, as owner of the Pendley estate, founded the Pendley Shakespeare Festival – to put on plays in the grounds of his home. The Festival has its origins in 1947 - some two years after Dorian Williams had helped to oversee the development of part of the Manor House at Pendley as a Residential Centre of Adult Education.

Grounds for Shakespeare.

At the end of July 1947, the Centre held an open day. All of the groups meeting regularly at Pendley under the Centre's auspices - including the Drama Group - displayed the results of their labours. In the Manor House gardens, the Drama Group presented some five or six scenes from Shakespeare's plays, including A Midsummer Night's Dream, King Richard II and Macbeth.

In the booklet 'Pendley Residential Centre of Adult Education, the first 25 years, 1945 – 1970' (published in

87

1970), the story is told that, by the interval at this first performance, the audience had grown tired of facing into the sun and, so, took the opportunity to move their chairs to the opposite side of the stage area. This meant that, for the second half of the play, it was the actors who had to face the now setting sun.

Nonetheless, this presentation was a success. So, the next year, the group performed famous love scenes from the Shakespearean canon – under the title of 'If music be the food of love...' using, for the first time, the 'Glade' stage. This is the stage in front of the path to the activity meadow - currently, where the Greek monuments are.

A scene from Henry VIII at Pendley in 1949. Photograph reproduced by permission.

The next year – 1949 – the Drama Group gave a full production of Shakespeare's Henry VIII and the Festival began. 1951 witnessed the first floodlit production and, by 1954, the Festival had become so successful that its organisers decided to present two productions: Julius

Caesar and A Midsummer Night's Dream. That set the pattern for each succeeding Festival.

Before 2001, most of the productions were presented on the Glade stage. This enabled actors (especially Dorian Williams) to make dramatic entrances on horseback down the glade. In 1962, 1963, 1964, 1968, 1970, 1980 and 1981, the Festival was presented using the 'Formal' stage. The Formal stage was a west-facing raised bank, over 80 feet (some 24.3 metres) wide which had a yew hedge background and was flanked by two 100 feet (some 30.4 metres) high Canadian fir trees. Characters would make their entrances and exits through the yew hedge.

A scene from a performance of King Lear, at Pendley, in 1986. John Branston plays Kent, John Tolputt is The Fool and Jim Smith is King Lear.

In 1989, while the Manor House was being converted into a hotel, a production of The Merchant of Venice was presented on a raised stage above the Rose Garden, on the north side of the Manor, with the Manor itself as a backdrop.

In 2001, Pendley Manor acquired a swimming pool and leisure centre. The electricity that this facility drew from the substation compromised the power that was available for the Festival.

In addition, increased demand for the Manor's wedding facilities, which were located within earshot of the Glade stage, meant that the Festival had to be downsized in terms of its power requirements and also relocated away from the wedding facilities. So the productions were moved to the 'Garden' – now known as 'The Williams' - stage. This stage is in front of a leafy bank, alongside the Rose Garden, and the audience seating is placed on the Manor's tennis courts.

Records show that, in the Festival's first 15 years, some 30,000 people had attended at least one of the Festival's 70 or so performances. Over 300 people had featured in the casts, and over 40 horses had taken part! Dorian Williams contrived to make at least a cameo appearance in most of the productions and, indeed, directed some of the earlier productions. His last appearance on stage in the Festival came in 1983. Dorian died in 1985 but – apart from 1988 when the Manor was being refurbished - the Festival has continued.

When Dorian Williams started the Shakespeare Festival, he brought in Ronnie Evers, Headmaster of Berkhamsted School, who continued to play comedy leads for many years. Given the timing of the Festival, it was natural for schoolteachers to be heavily involved. Incidentally, the Festival also received some help from Ronnie Evers' sister, Sybil Evers who, for many years, played leading parts in the operas of Gilbert & Sullivan, for the D'Oyly Carte Opera Company.

From Repton, Michael Charlesworth came to play tragic leads and direct and, from the Leys, Stephen Siddall. A Festival Director, David Sherratt, followed Ronnie Evers from Berkhamsted. Andrew Boxer came from Eastbourne.

Whitgift, in Surrey, sent John Branston. Jennie spotted him and romantically asked Marjorie Evers (Ronnie Evers' wife), "Who's the bald bloke with the big nose?"

In all sorts of roles, both John and Jennie Branston were part of 46 festivals. John gave his last performance at Pendley in 2013, ending in the same Shakespearian part as he began. John and Jennie produced Sarah Branston, who is now Director of Drama at Reigate Grammar School. She first appeared on the Pendley stage at the age of seven, progressed via acting and directing, and is the current Artistic Director of the Festival.

The tradition goes on. 2013 brought Peter Broad from Eton to direct the Festival.

The Festival personnel rely on strong personal connections and there are many family traditions associated with the Festival. An Aldbury family, the Ellwoods, have provided three generations of support.

Caroline helped Dorian Williams with set design. Her children, Tobias (a former captain in The Royal Green Jackets who has gone on to become a Conservative MP), Jonathan (who, at the time he was killed in the Bali bombing in 2002, was the Director of Studies at the International School in Ho Chi Minh City in Vietnam) and Totty, performing - and, now, her grandchildren, Felicity and Freddie, are taking on ensemble roles.

Danny Murphy has provided the technical support for the Festival for over 20 years. Over the years, set design and construction has been provided by the Randall family - brothers Bob and Derek building ambitious constructions for productions, with help from friends and family.

The Festival even provides romance, as John and Jennie Branston's story illustrates. Bob Randall also met his wife, Lynda, while she was coordinating props for productions - and they got married at the Pendley Manor Hotel.

The Festival company of players is re-formed each year, although several of its members return year after year. While many are talented amateurs, others go on to have successful professional acting careers. These include:

- **Lynda Bellingham**, who appeared in plays at the Pendley Festival twice during the 1960s. Despite making many television appearances, Lynda is probably best known as the head of the family in the Oxo television adverts during the 1980s.

- **Stephen Campbell Moore**, who featured on stage and screen in Alan Bennett's The History Boys.

- **Raza Jaffrey**, formerly Zafar Younis in BBC Television's Spooks, and Butler Gaurav in the film, Sex and the City 2.

- **Caroline Quentin**, who first achieved fame as Dorothy in the television series, Men Behaving Badly, and went on to play Maddy Magellan in the Jonathan Creek programmes.

- **Hermione Norris**, who played Carol Jordan in the crime drama series, Wire in the Blood, before joining the cast of BBC TV's Spooks as Ros Myers and, later, performing alongside Stephen Fry in the ITV comedy drama, Kingdom.

The Shakespeare Festival allows the current Artistic Director to provide some of her finest students with opportunities to develop their theatrical skills.

A past student, Tom Attwood, ran the Festival with Sarah Branston. Subsequently, Tom has gone on to perform at the National Theatre and has developed a successful artistic career as a Musical Director.

Another pupil, Helen Mumby, took over from Tom Attwood as the Shakespeare Festival Director and is currently developing her career as a theatrical agent.

A former pupil, Will Edwards, has now assumed the role of Festival producer alongside Sarah Branston. Sarah's past pupils have performed while training at Drama School and still return in a professional capacity to perform, stage manage and direct.

While the Festival began as an amateur event, professional actors now perform alongside actors from the local community. Performing two plays by Shakespeare in the glorious grounds, to over 600 people each night for two weeks is a huge treat for professional actors.

The artistic team rehearse for a gruelling 14 hours a day, but get to stay at the glorious four star hotel, with all the facilities and hospitality that such a hotel offers. The relationship between the hotel management and the artistic collective is always excellent. The hotel sponsorship of the Festival, alongside the professional skill of each year's theatrical company continues to provide a hugely successful theatrical event for local arts lovers.

A scene from the early days of Shakespeare at Pendley.

With regards to staging Shakespeare at Pendley, the last word should go to the Festival's founder, Dorian Williams.

In his book, 'Pendley and a Pack of Hounds', he wrote: 'It is not difficult to hold the attention of an audience unused to sitting through a full-length Shakespeare play, with so much to interest them and rivet the eye and ear.

'The distant cawing of rooks, as Macbeth invokes the powers of darkness; the drifting spirals of smoke ruddied by the glow from friendly braziers as Henry V wanders through his camp; the great cedars sighing and swaying as

94

Lear battles with the storm; a huge harvest moon behind the parapets throwing little Arthur into tragic silhouette before he plunges to his death; the vicious glare in the sky from a mighty bonfire showing Antony's words have found their target and the conspirators' houses have, indeed, been burned.

'And "A Midsummer Night's Dream": a green bank, a hidden dell, a glade some hundred yards long. Here, surely, is fairyland personified.'

Rehearsal...

... and performance.

A scene from the early days of Shakespeare at Pendley.

A scene from the early days of Shakespeare at Pendley.

A scene from the early days of Shakespeare at Pendley.

More scenes from the early days of Shakespeare at Pendley...

Appendix: A personal perspective of Pendley

Having first sampled – and been enthralled by - the delights of Pendley Manor many years ago when, as a child, I visited its Shakespeare Festival, I'm always keen to find any excuse to re-visit Pendley. Pendley – which offers some echoes of the above stairs lifestyle of a latter day 'Downton Abbey' – can provide a glimpse of late-Victorian gracious living but with the facilities now expected of a modern country house hotel.

A glimpse of late-Victorian gracious living but with the facilities now expected of a modern country house hotel.

A recent visit was for some relaxation one winter weekend.

After checking in, my wife (Helen) and I found our way to our room – a large room in the more modern part of the hotel. The room not only had its own dining table, settee, coffee table and dressing table but it also featured a superking sized bed that, from its ample width, looked like it was made for three rather than two people. Other rooms – particularly in the original house – have four poster beds but not so many dining and coffee tables.

The bed looked like it was made for three rather than two people.

Other rooms have four poster beds.

The next task was to go in search of a cup of tea – which was easily accomplished in the leather armchaired splendour of the Shakespeare Bar. Over the ornate giant Victorian fireplace there was a newly erected certificate, reassuringly proclaiming that Pendley had been highly commended in the 'large hotel/ townhouse of the year' category of The Beautiful South Awards, organised by Tourism South East.

The Shakespeare Bar.

Edified and fortified, we set about researching the hotel's leisure facilities. In the bowels of the old building – once upon a time, the cellars – is an archetypal country house snooker room and a gym. The gym is more than adequate for the casual 'keep fitter' and, judging from its other occupant on our visit, it's suitable for the serious workout fanatic too.

We met our gym partner again a little while later, in the much newer swimming pool complex, sampling the effects of an instant flatulence machine otherwise known as a spa bath. Connected to the pool area by a subterranean passage are the sauna and steam rooms. We found that a visit to these then necessitated a trip to the instant flatulence machine in order to chill out.

The snooker room...

... and gym.

The swimming pool complex – with the instant flatulence machine in the foreground.

To the delight of those who don't want to - or feel they daren't - chill out too much at Pendley, the hotel provides free wi-fi access which even a technophobe, such as me, should find easy to access.

The evening heralded our eagerly awaited dinner appointment in the restaurant. Experience has taught us that the quality of the food at Pendley is excellent. This time, we chose from the à la carte menu:

To start

Red Ace, Ruby Queen and Burpie Beetroot, Goat Cheese & Blush Tomato Mousse, Silverskins, Crisps Bob Bobs and Glazed Chanteney Carrots (a vegetarian option), and

Aylesbury Duck and Squab Pigeon Terrine, Celeste Figs, Watercress Crème Fraiche, Golden Raisins, Fried Brioche

Mains

Loin of 50 Day Aged Ashridge (local) Venison rolled in Hazelnut and Juniper, Butternut Squash, Parmentier Potato and Bombay Sapphire Jus (A wine recommendation, from the Pendley cellar, would be Brown Brothers Limited Release Heathcote Shiraz, Victoria, Australia 2008)

Butter Poached Halibut Fillet, Chive Mash, Caramelised Veal Breads, Gem Lettuce Morels, Green Beans, Jerez Vinegar Skied Chicken Stock (Pendley would recommend: Reisling, Straser Weinberge, Martin Arndorfer, Austria 2006)

Dessert

Hot lemon soufflé, Raspberry Sorbet, Vanilla Shortbread

Hot Chocolate Fondant 70% Cocoa, Pistachio Ice Cream

We included a large bottle of sparkling Decante Spring water (from Conwy in North Wales) and began the meal not just with some bread rolls but also with two nicely blended St Clements (a combination of orange juice and bitter lemon). Afterwards, I had some coffee - Helen preferred hot chocolate - and there were petit fours.

In the English country house tradition, breakfast the next morning – as every viewer of 'Gosford Park' and 'Downton Abbey' knows – is a self-service meal with an almost confusing array of options. I chose cereals, followed by bacon, scrambled eggs and, to my mind, a key determinant of the quality of any hotel's breakfast table, freshly cooked tomatoes. Again, Pendley's chefs easily passed the test. Helen was more adventurous in terms of the cooked breakfast options but came to same conclusion as I had.

In the restaurant.

There was also tea (for me) and coffee (for Helen) accompanied – in the manner of Enid Blyton's stories – by lashings of toast and preserves.

Since it was winter, although the weather was bright, we didn't feel intrepid enough to brave the elements and trek around the 35 acres of the Pendley estate, much of which is woodland. In the better weather, however, the Manor's gardens and grounds - about a 40 minute train journey from London - provide welcome havens of rural peace.

From time to time, however, the peace of Pendley's grounds is shattered by the call of the Manor's tribe of ten or so peacocks/ peahens. They tend to roost in the big beech tree close to the house but they roam the grounds, getting into whatever mischief they can. Apparently, they'll deign to appear in wedding photographs – or not – in inverse correlation with whether or not you want them to.

A chat with the duty manager, revealed that Pendley's two baby peacocks had recently been given to a local farmer, after their mother had been killed by a fox.

106

A Pendley peacock.

He explained: "The adult peacocks roost in the big trees here – out of the way of foxes - but the young birds stay on the ground and hide. One morning, however, we found the youngsters but the peahen had died defending them."

Pendley's last private owner, Dorian Williams, left two major legacies for us all. One was his grade II listed country house and its grounds. The other legacy comes to life every summer. At the end of the Second World War, Dorian turned his home, Pendley Manor, into an adult education centre. Two years later, one of the centre's groups performed some scenes from Shakespeare plays in the Manor grounds and, two years after that, the Pendley Shakespeare Festival began.

A fine picnic at Pendley.

Every August, the Manor's grounds are turned into an open air theatrical Glyndebourne, as picnickers party in the summer evening sun before enjoying a dose of Shakespearean culture. While rain is not unheard of in Tring, it's rare during the Festival, so there's a good chance of combining a fine picnic with a fine evening's entertainment.